30 Beautiful Things

That Are True About You

*A collection of thoughts
about all the things that
make you so great!*

Douglas Pagels

Blue Mountain Press

Boulder, Colorado

Library of Congress Control Number: 2004112879
ISBN: 978-0-88396-881-9

Certain trademarks are used under license.
BLUE MOUNTAIN PRESS is registered in U.S. Patent and Trademark Office.

Printed in the United States of America.
Fourth Printing: 2007

 This book is printed on recycled paper.

This book is printed on fine quality, laid embossed, 80 lb. paper. This paper has been specially produced to be acid free (neutral pH) and contains no groundwood or unbleached pulp. It conforms with all the requirements of the American National Standards Institute, Inc., so as to ensure that this book will last and be enjoyed by future generations.

Blue Mountain Arts, Inc.

P.O. Box 4549, Boulder, Colorado 80306

"People who
have great things
within them
have wonderful things
in store for them.

May your todays
and your tomorrows
be a beautiful reflection
of all that you are."

— Douglas Pagels

You are
appreciated
and celebrated.

I want you to feel really good...
about who you are.
About all the great things you do!
Acknowledge your talents and
abilities. Realize what a beautiful
person you are.

Who knew! that the high
school football jock had
such amazing culinary skills
waiting to be friend!

You are
quietly thanked for
so many things.

I want you to understand that your presence is a present to the world. And I hope you will be sure to remember the things that are so endearing, so impressive, and so true... about you.

You are truly a gift!

You are
an inspiration.

Among all the great things you do,
you are capable of...
Reaching down deep and searching
within. Discovering how strong you can
be. Rising up as high as a wishing star.
And loving the possibilities you see.

You are such
an amazing
person.

You're a one-of-a-kind gift to this space and time. You're the only one in the universe exactly like you! I want you to take care of that rare and remarkable soul. You deserve it.

You are blessed.

You know that it's easy to invest in
the best riches of all, and that precious
moments are most likely to come to
those who search them out.

You know that cherished times are to be found in heart-to-heart conversations, and that you can have a wealth of beautiful tomorrows... just by moving ahead of any worries, moving beyond any sorrows, and using the present to shape the future.

You are
insightful.

You know how important it is to...
Believe in yourself.
Be the miracle you are.
Let the wonder in.
Let all the worries out.

You are a free spirit,
my son, which scares
the hell out of me some
times. And I wish I
was more like you.

You are someone with great potential.

You have the ability to make every day special. Each new morning comes to us gift-wrapped, and fresh out of the box are moments we've never experienced before, opportunities we've never known, and chances we've never taken.

What a truly magnificent gift! Those with the "same-old, same-old" outlook let the chances just slip away. But those who understand the value of the gift? Well... they have a chance to turn the present... into a really extraordinary day!

You are
caring
and creative.

You have the ability to...
Follow your heart.
Trust your instincts.
Listen to the song that sings in you.
And let your spirit dance to that tune.

You know
the value of
the best treasures.

You know that although it's important to have enough material wealth to meet your needs, loved ones and friends are the real treasures of life, and happiness is the real wealth.

Life is precious... and it's too short to spend it trying to accumulate things that, in the end, will pale in comparison to possessing peace of mind. Aim for the best level of health you can achieve, a place where you truly feel at home, feelings that make you feel so alive, the smiles your favorite memories can bring, and all those things of immense value... that will never have price tags on them.

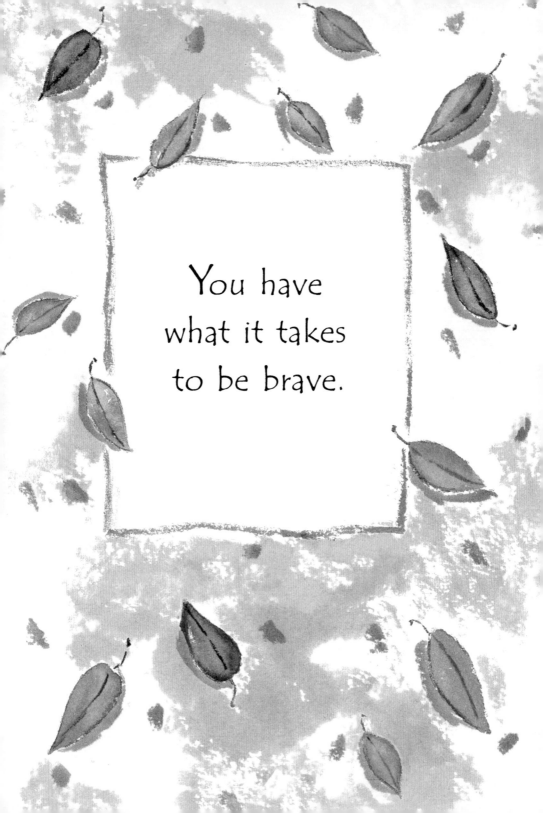

You have
what it takes
to be brave.

You can remember: it's all about choices.
Realize: the decisions are up to you.
And never forget: you're in the driver's
seat, and you can travel through life
in any direction you choose.

You hold tomorrow within your hands.

The way there will be shared with so many things: hopes and wishes. Prayers and dreams. The strength to meet your challenges. The courage to continue on. The ability to benefit from the truths of yesterday (be they good or bad).

The many qualities you've spent a lifetime developing. The inner gifts you've always had. Your very own roadmap to happiness. The personal path you take. The compass that comes from listening to your heart. And the journey... you lovingly make.

You have a life
that is filled with
opportunities.

I want you to know that there is
someone who will thank you for
doing the things you do now with
foresight and wisdom and respect.
It's the person you will someday be.

I want you to make that
person so thankful and so proud.

*You're on your way, Scott.
Be the most you can be!*

You are
a shining example.

Every star is important to the sky.
You're here to shine in your own
special way. May you never forget
how essential and how rare you are.

I want you to be sure to never lose your
sense of wonder... and to hold on to your
sense of humor, the sparkle in your eyes,
and the warmhearted way that you
brighten your corner of the world.

You brighten my corner of the world!

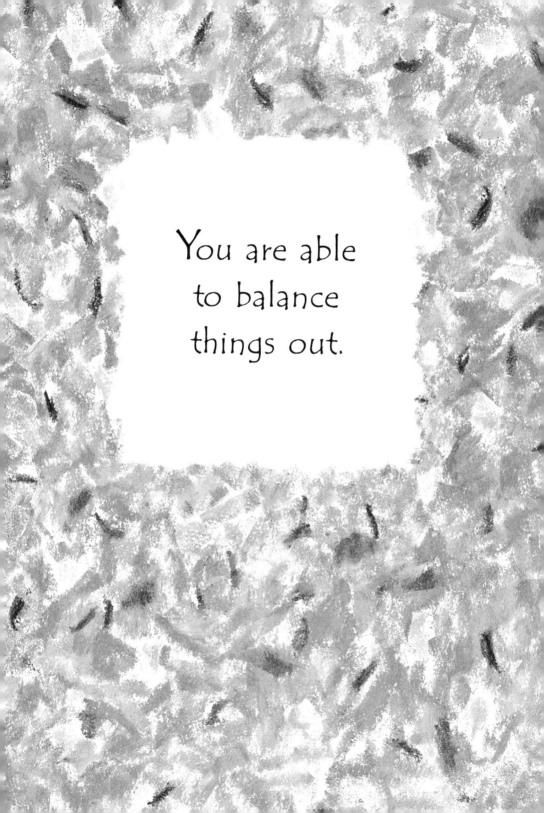

You are able
to balance
things out.

You know that life doesn't always play by the rules, but in the long run, everything will work out okay. You understand that you and your actions are capable of turning anything around — and that joys once lost can always be found again.

You have had so many trials and tribulations and still have that wonderful smile to share. You always make it through the tough times. Hang in there. It's worth it. You're worth it

You are someone everyone should admire.

There are many things to admire about you, but one of the nicest is that you do the things you do with an inner strength and a special kind of love.

That's just the way you are. You give life a gleam that most people only carry a glimpse of.

You have
an appreciation for
the finer things
in life.

You appreciate honesty. Understanding. Trust. Closeness. Openness. Support. Giving. Receiving. Believing. Family. Home. Making memories. Keeping in touch. New friends. Old friends. Good work. Fun times. Favorite shows and books and songs. Communication. Tolerance. Kind people. The sky above. The earth below. Laughter. Light. And love.

You know that — if you need to — you can always make a change.

You know that life is filled with options. You can travel in the direction of those things that will make your heart glad.

It may take awhile. And you may need to deal with things you'd rather not dwell on. But if you want it bad enough, your courage will carry you to a brighter day. There is always a way… to get to the place where you can live the life you've always wanted to have.

You will
make it through
whatever
comes along.

Mom

"May troubles, worries, and problems never linger; may they only make you that much stronger and able and wise. May you rise each day with sunlight in your heart, success in your path, answers to your prayers, and that smile — that I love to see — always there in your eyes."

I wish this with all my heart. You have had your share but you always find your way back on top. Keep climbing, my son.

You have
so much
going for you.

You are a special person, and you
have a future that is in the best of
hands. And you need to remember:

If you have plans you want to act on
and dreams you've always wanted to
come true, you have what it takes,
because no matter what you want to
do... you have the help of someone
who can try and reach and achieve
just about anything. You are so lucky
because... you have you.

You are Awesome

You are
sensitive to
the needs
of others.

I love your smile!

Keep sharing your smile. You always make people see things in a brighter light. You are here to shine in your own wonderful way, remembering all the while that a little light somewhere makes a brighter light everywhere.

Smiles are contagious

You are fortunate to have so many choices.

Everywhere you go, every day. In everything you do, you come to a crossroads. And what will it be? This way or that... this road? This path?

Stay true to yourself.
Remember the lessons you
have learned throughout
your life's journey.
Don't sacrifice

All the things you choose to do
reflect... on your ability, your
integrity, your spirit, your health,
your tomorrows, your smiles, your
dreams, and yourself. It's not that
hard to have a wealth of beautiful
tomorrows. All you have to do is...
choose wisely.

You have a
big heart and
a fascinating
mind.

Keep your heart filled with happiness
and keep finding new ways to grow.
Keep yearning. Keep learning.
Keep trying. Keep smiling. *you have an*
And keep remembering that *amazing smile!*
so many hopes and wishes go
with you everywhere you go.

You are deserving of every good thing that can come your way.

You know it's not an easy world we live in. And that difficulties arise in the lives of us all. We have to be realistic, sure. But that doesn't mean we have to be pessimistic.

We have to be safe and smart and cautious, absolutely. But that doesn't mean we have to be afraid. In life, as in love, the jewels come to those who are willing to take the chances, stay open to the possibilities, keep the faith, and just do what it takes to make it work.

You have
so many
possibilities
ahead.

Keep the door open. Okay, that's good, but just a little wider. There. Now, remember: good things come to good people, and you're one of the best. So don't be too quick to limit your choices of what to do, because in doing so, you might limit your chances of unimagined joys that are waiting just for you.

You are
the leader of
your own life.

You realize the need to go out of your way to stay healthy in body and soul, and to deal with the stress of living in what is sometimes a difficult world.

When you listen carefully, you instinctively know when to work your mind and let your body relax, and when doing just the opposite makes the most sense. You know that being able to handle whatever life brings your way is not a matter of coincidence.

You are
worthy of
so much
recognition.

I want the people who share your days to realize that they are in the presence of a very special person. Keep understanding that the world could use more outstanding people like you.

You have some amazing friends and I know they love you and appreciate the person you are.

'Love One Another'

You will always be in my heart.

No matter what is happening
  in the world.
No matter what worries or
  frustrations creep in.
No matter what glad or sad tidings
  come your way.
No matter how many bills come
  in the mail.

No matter how good or bad the
news of the day.
No matter whether the weather is
beautiful or not.
No matter how many times your
smile gets lost.
No matter how difficult or
demanding things can be.
No matter what is happening
anywhere at any time…
you will be in my thoughts
and warmest wishes.

You really are only a thought
away and I miss you more
than you know. But know
that you are in the place
you need to be – in my heart
for ever and ever!

You are
a very
generous
and giving
person.

You give <u>so many</u> people a reason to
smile. You deserve to receive the best
in return, and one of my heart's favorite
hopes is that the happiness you give away
will come back to warm you each and
every day of your life.

So many people tell me what
a great guy you are and how
much the love you... I begin
with pride... My heart
swells. Never change, Sweetheart!

You know what it's all about.

You know that it's all about making the most of your life and of the time you have been given. About doing the best you can do — and letting go of the things that are beyond your control. It's about believing in tomorrow and stretching your wings. Embracing your blessings and appreciating all the sweet memories you've made.

It's about reaching for your dreams, brightening your days, and filling your heart in a thousand ways. It's about lifting up others, sharing the load, and continuing down the road on the way to making things better than they were before.

It's about having as few regrets as possible — and more things to smile about than you ever imagined. It's about being a deserving person, whether you get recognized for your wonderful qualities or not. It's about knowing that people like you help to tip the balance away from the people who are unkind and uncaring, and that you are an essential part of the grace that comes from good people everywhere.

It's about envisioning how things should be. Always being part of the solution. Never part of the problem. Being crystal clear about the importance of integrity and not letting other people blur the boundaries. It's about believing in just causes, just because they need all the help they can get.

It's about knowing that the world begins at your doorstep and goes outward from there. It's about you standing there, taking it all in, realizing that you are part of a remarkable moment in time... and that nothing can get in the way of the opportunities that shine as brightly as the heavens above.

It's about being happy to be alive, fortunate to be able to feel and see and learn and help and heal and give and grow. It's about being so lucky to share a friendship and to have someone to love. It's about doing what you can while you can and knowing that it's never too late... ever. It's about having steppingstones to look forward to, milestones to look back upon and, in between, being part of a grand scheme of connect-the-dot-days that lead the way to success.

It's about rolling up your sleeves, tying on your traveling shoes, and taking the next step into whatever lies ahead.

You must
never forget
what a treasure
you are.

That special person in the mirror
may not always get to hear all the
compliments you so sweetly deserve,
but you are so worthy of
such an abundance
of friendship, joy,
and love.

And I do love you!
Mom.

About the Author

Bestselling author and editor Douglas Pagels has inspired millions of readers with his insights and his anthologies. No one is better at touching on so many subjects that are deeply personal and truly universal at the same time.

His writings have been translated into seven languages due to their global appeal and inspiring outlook on life, and his work has been quoted by many worthy causes and charitable organizations.

He and his wife live in Colorado, and they are the parents of children in high school and college. Over the years, Doug has spent much of his time as a classroom volunteer, a youth basketball coach, an advocate for local environmental issues, a frequent traveler, and a craftsman, building a cabin in the Rocky Mountains.